VIVID   VAGUE

VIVID & VAGUE

MARC GEFFEN

DEPTH
DEPT.

BROOKLYN NEW YORK

FIRST DEPTH DEPARTMENT EDITION, APRIL 2014

```
D E P T H
D E P T .
```

ISBN-10: 0615987702
ISBN-13: 978-0615987705

www.depthdepartment.com

FOR

Friends who are family
and family who are friends

CONTENTS

INTRODUCTION

These things, man. These kinds of things just creep up. All of a sudden I became eerily conscious of my consciousness, and the past came into focus: years and layers of untruth fortified by time and ubiquity, my perspective drenched in the wake of prior thinkers like a dirtied lens.

I had uncovered foreignness at a hyper-local level, but confirmed no intruder; this, one in a series of incisive syllogisms, catalyzed the end of a certain era of *me*. Shit was about to hit the fan, but I took solace in the fact that at least I would no longer be full of shit. I should document this, I thought, and ultimately may not have had a choice in the matter. Sometimes curiosity demands to keep a record of itself.

Vivid & Vague is a collection of cuts from that record, curated and shared with the view that self-help is an organic, philosophical practice - not a genre. Beyond the written word and its digital transmissions, Vivid & Vague is a state of mind for a mind that's learning to be comfortable while not knowing - you know, not *really* knowing - what state it's in.

REALITY   TRUTH

Life is a collection of vivid experiences and memories that compose the terrain of a vague reality.

Emotions provide the atmosphere in which this reality thrives. Without emotions the land-scape is simply a backdrop, though not devoid of beauty.

Like blood
that rushes to a wound and clots,
we fill the void of our reality
with meaning.

You are a projection. To alter the projected image, adjust the source of light.

Yes, follow the flow of life. Without conscious disruption, though, life can become a
stagnant pond.

Instead, incite momentum in flow by creating
ripples in the pond to carry you outward.

Life gives us natural balance: good + bad. We spend this life trying to tip the scale, but isn't balance perfect?

A STORY OF TRUTH

He liked to sit in the heat – in the absence of air conditioning during humid New York summers, or on the beach as his skin baked under the South Jersey sun – and sip ice water, deliberately letting beads of cold liquid dribble from his chin and funnel down his abdomen like a freshwater spring, all the water collecting in the basin of his belly button. It felt a bit queer and slightly primitive, yet he enjoyed the feeling of the cool stream with unabashed purity, just as he loved the touch of a woman's delicate fingers tickling the skin on his back. It was a fusion of function and indulgence, this bizarre drooling method, the icy water cooling his fiery temperament and the absurdity of the act allowing him to view life as a timeline of triviality extending for miles in both directions.

FEAR   PAIN

Logic is like a type of math in which variables take on values derived from intuition.

Optimizing the life you lead has nothing to do with adding variables to the equation. It's about testing - and subsequently rejecting - constraints.

The greatest thing about life is that it unfolds as a series of choices and we may learn to control how we perceive the outcomes of those choices.

Preferences pervade the cracks in our perception; we will certainly experience things as bad or unfortunate.

When we realize, however, that our experience of something as bad is simply a conditioned interpretation, we begin to recognize the divergence of preference and truth: the former, a parasite disguised as the latter.

Your fear consists of fear and only fear.
This may seem an intuitive characterization,
but sometimes the most obvious is also the
most beautiful:

Fear is a one-trick pony.

It wears a formidable face, but fear is always
on the ropes, infected by its own sickness.
Fear itself is scared, intrinsically fearful,
and only fearful.

Take the pony for a ride. Understand that fear
cannot be destroyed because fear is energy. It
must be channeled and converted.

Time warps at an inverse relationship to our desire. When enjoying oneself, time speeds up, devouring the present more quickly. When in pain and one wishes time would move fast, it downshifts, trudging along, a phenomenon of meticulousness. No wonder we can't divert our eyes from the clock of life.

A STORY OF PAIN

I am seeing a psychologist. We've been dating for three months, so I *see* her, naked. Great tits, mediocre legs and ass, PhD. She probably won't last - I'm an ass man - but it's nice to know that she's smart and her smart self finds me appealing.

Trust me, though: you don't need to pick up an attractive, young psychologist at a bar and pretend you might love her for three months because the skirt suits she wears turn you on and so does the prospect of in-house therapy.

Nope. Didn't need her.* Without her analysis I came to realize I am not unlike anyone else, no more or less afflicted by what may be the most powerful drug known to man: relief. Relief is addictive yet perceived as tepid; no one seems to notice its potency. It's almost undetectable as a dope. Relief's clever disguise is that anxiety sets in first as a preconditioned side effect, leading us to experience the comedown before the ecstasy.

* Writing this, I remember a college friend who studied psychology before switching his major to mathematics because, as he put it, "sanity is too subjective."

LOVE   TRUST

Love feeds your ego;
true love cuts its throat.

In love, the rhythms of life synchronize. Waves crash on the shore of each soul at the same time.

Withstand the tides and enjoy the occasional flood. You asked for it.

The world we live in is the product of an interference pattern, the sum of our individual experiences colliding.

Set your experiences on a collision course with others'; trust that course, and you multiply the scope of your world.

Life changes for the better if you let yourself be selective when it comes to the company you keep.

One of the greatest expressions of free will is to choose to surround yourself with those who make you feel most free.

A STORY OF LOVE

She wore a nice sweater. By "nice" I mean the way it felt, not its fashion or its fit. It felt nice on my cheek as I buried my face in her chest, listening to the sounds of life pulse beneath the refuge of her cleavage. Her heart was bleeding, but in a healthy way, within a controlled system. Mine bled uncontrollably.

This is me as a grown man, an ostrich with its head in the sand. I thought about waiting it out. Maybe it would pass. Maybe I would just bleed out in her arms, becoming a puddle of lifeless juice, leaving my mark on this world as a grotesque stain on her top. I didn't give a fuck about how it looked anyway; I gave so few fucks about those details that I'm not even going to tell you about the color or style of her sweater. In that moment - in that period of my life, actually - all I cared about was pure substance, the fabric of everything. And that grandiose, reaching-for-meaning approach was killing me.

She was my lover and my confidant. Her embrace mollified, like a pillow feathered with all the happy memories of my past, a pillow I could cry into without shame. I did. I cried and let the tears soak her sweater, leaving just a temporary stain. The permanence of blood would have to wait. I decided right then and there that I had more life to live.

CULTURE   CREATIVITY

The counterculture is the culture
that you count on.

Personality is an aesthetic. It's not so much a natural incandescence of identity as it is the design of an essence, a way of emitting the heat of living through the controlled glow of a very specific hue.

We look at others' work - their poems, films, comedy, music - and consider it art hatched from anomalous inspiration. It is something they do to "express" themselves, a translation of their feelings and ideas, a creative representation of their singular ego.

Actually, these efforts are much more collective in nature, examples of a communal exercise to make sense of the world by making an impression upon it. While nuanced, they're not so individualistic. We all do it, we all do this.

It's a matter of style, really.

Contentment ≠ complacency.
Complacency kills.

A STORY OF CREATIVITY

I was told recently that I am a "well adjusted young man." I understand what he meant; we were having somewhat of a philosophical conversation and I mentioned something about seeking truth without pushing our problems onto others at the expense of their psychological fitness. But I am not well adjusted. I am constantly adjusting. I have not reached a state of correction or a place called "there." Any shifts I have made are not complete and never will be.

All I know is I'm feeling really good right now because I've found the elusive enzyme that converts inspiration into optimism, and I've successfully harnessed that little fucker.

THE FUTURE

There is not much to say here. We are all forever green and will lack much of the understanding we assume is fermenting in our future.

Foresight is the punk younger brother of wisdom.

www.ingramcontent.com/pod-product-compliance
Lightning Source LLC
Chambersburg PA
CBHW070206060426
42445CB00033B/1758